AN IDEAS INTO ACTION GUIDE

Feedback in Performance Reviews

IDEAS INTO ACTION GUIDEBOOKS

Aimed at managers and executives who are concerned with their own and others' development, each guidebook in this series gives specific advice on how to complete a developmental task or solve a leadership problem.

LEAD CONTRIBUTOR	E. Wayne Hart
CONTRIBUTORS	John Fleenor
	Pete Hammett
	Bertrand Sereno
	Stephanie Trovas
	Jim Wilson

DIRECTOR OF ASSESSMENTS, TOOLS, AND PUBLICATIONS	Sylvester Taylor
MANAGER, PUBLICATION DEVELOPMENT	Peter Scisco
EDITOR	Stephen Rush
EDITOR	Karen Lewis
DESIGN AND LAYOUT	Joanne Ferguson
CONTRIBUTING ARTISTS	Laura J. Gibson
	Chris Wilson, 29 & Company

CCL No. 450
ISBN No. 978-1-60491-114-5

CENTER FOR CREATIVE LEADERSHIP
WWW.CCL.ORG

AN IDEAS INTO ACTION GUIDEBOOK

Feedback in Performance Reviews

E. Wayne Hart

Center for
Creative
Leadership

THE IDEAS INTO ACTION GUIDEBOOK SERIES

This series of guidebooks draws on the practical knowledge that the Center for Creative Leadership (CCL®) has generated, since its inception in 1970, through its research and educational activity conducted in partnership with hundreds of thousands of managers and executives. Much of this knowledge is shared—in a way that is distinct from the typical university department, professional association, or consultancy. CCL is not simply a collection of individual experts, although the individual credentials of its staff are impressive; rather it is a community, with its members holding certain principles in common and working together to understand and generate practical responses to today's leadership and organizational challenges.

The purpose of the series is to provide managers with specific advice on how to complete a developmental task or solve a leadership challenge. In doing that, the series carries out CCL's mission to advance the understanding, practice, and development of leadership for the benefit of society worldwide. We think you will find the Ideas Into Action Guidebooks an important addition to your leadership toolkit.

Table of Contents

EXECUTIVE BRIEF

Effective feedback is one of the most important components of successful performance reviews. Feedback is assessment data that either supports continuing to perform in some manner or targets a desirable change. This guidebook will help you provide performance review feedback that will be well received. It explains three feedback principles and four different types of feedback. Each of these four types is effective when used at the right time and for the right reasons, and they can be used in combination. This guidebook will help you understand when to use the different types of feedback and how to frame a complete feedback message. The rest is practice.

Feedback Gone Awry

Brenda was an enthusiastic, bright, and talented computer technician. Her manager, Ethan, saw a great future for her at the Community Health Center, where she supported medical staff in the Women's Health Department. Despite Brenda's track record of quickly solving system user problems, there had been complaints about her "brash" attitude. Her internal customers felt belittled by her use of phrases like "user error," "what's your problem?" and "why didn't you...?"

At their annual performance review, Ethan coached Brenda with a little feedback on how to better word things. "Instead of 'user error,' try saying, 'entry glitch.'"

"I don't see why I should have to mince words," she protested. "They don't listen to me anyway. They don't want to learn anything— they just want a quick fix."

Ethan was more than a little discouraged by Brenda's defensiveness, but he recognized that her edgy response to him was exactly the type of behavior that was alienating the medical staff. He tried another approach, explaining, "It's about customer service. Try speaking in their language. For example, instead of asking, 'What is your problem with the computer?' ask, 'What are the symptoms?'"

"I've told some of them three or four times that they have to reenter their pass codes, and they won't do it. Their attitude is the problem!" Brenda was becoming more agitated. Ethan wanted to calm her down and get back to the subject.

"Brenda, you're one of the sharpest problem solvers on the team. But if you don't improve your reputation with the medical staff, I will be forced to make some changes."

"Now you're threatening *me*," Brenda exclaimed, "when *their* laziness is the problem? Why should I have to make the changes?"

Ethan's discouragement was now joined by a sense of being cornered. He did not have a "next move" in mind, so he asked Brenda to think about it and adjourned the meeting, scheduling a follow-up conversation for the next week.

Ethan's encounter with Brenda is all too common. He thoughtfully offered her advice on how to act in the future. Yet Brenda was argumentative and defensive. Behind such behavior she likely felt offended, hurt, threatened, or angry, whether or not she was aware of it. She interpreted the situation exclusively from her own point of view. She did not understand what members of the medical staff experienced when she said things to them in certain ways. Brenda lacked self-awareness, an understanding of how she had behaved, and a realization of the impact that her behavior had on others. She did not receive Ethan's feedback well, and a developmental opportunity turned into a stalemate. How could Ethan have handled it better?

Reviewing Performance Reviews

At the Center for Creative Leadership, we often hear complaints about performance reviews. If an employee is meeting or exceeding expectations, reviews likely offer no substantial developmental direction. If an employee's performance falls short of expectations, corrective advice typically focuses on specific tasks. Sometimes, issues are not honestly addressed or are totally avoided, clarity about needed improvement is not established, and support for change is absent. Often, developmental and performance goals are not differentiated, or one of the two will be absent from the review. Common employee complaints about performance reviews include the following:

- "It's just a ritual; I don't get anything out of it. We're just checking off the boxes."

- "I just agree with everything, wait for it to be over, and then go out and do the best I can."
- "I never come out of the review feeling motivated."
- "I was judged against goals that were never made clear to me in the beginning."

Reviewers complain too. Their common complaints include the following:

- "I hate having to confront people on underperformance because they get upset or defensive."
- "I think we have set corrections in motion, but then nothing changes."
- "I know that either I am overly direct or I talk around the issue without really making the point."
- "It feels more like combat than working together for everyone's benefit."

One remedy for these problems is effective feedback. In fact, effective feedback is one of the most important components of successful performance reviews. Quality performance review feedback engages the employee in the conversation, informs the employee as to why expectations and goals are set as they are, clarifies priorities, aids measurement of progress or regression, increases awareness of how the employee is perceived by others in the organization, and highlights the organizational results of the employee's behavior.

In CCL's work with organizational leaders and managers, we have found that giving effective feedback to others is one of the most important skills for any leader or manager to master. Often it is one of the most difficult skills to apply consistently and well. Many leaders and managers have told us that they would far rather receive feedback about themselves than give feedback to someone else. And most senior leaders indicate that they want more feedback than they receive; this problem is greater the higher in the organization the leader operates.

The Role of Feedback in a Review

Performance reviews vary from one organization to the next. In some settings they serve compliance and legalistic needs, in others they are used to drive performance, and in still others they are part of a talent development process. Sometimes the "annual review" is the only feedback an organizational member gets; other times goals are set at the beginning of a period, feedback is given along the way at frequent intervals, and the end-of-the-period performance review contains no surprises, celebrates progress, and sets new goals. There are many other ways in which reviews differ. This guidebook respects that different review processes are appropriate for different organizations and individuals. Our topic here is a small part of the performance review landscape; it is how to use feedback in whatever performance review context you find yourself.

Feedback is important assessment data that either supports continuing to perform in some manner or targets a desirable change in how one performs (doing more or less of something). Performance reviews with no feedback fail to present the argument for making a change, pursuing a goal, or keeping things as they are. They fail to demonstrate the urgency or importance of expectations and goals. And they fail to highlight and reinforce desirable behavior. Performance reviews with poorly delivered feedback create bad feelings, discomfort, distrust, and disengagement.

When you give effective feedback, the feedback receiver learns something useful and feels supported in continuing a kind of action or in taking different actions in the future; ineffective feedback adds no learning and fails to support continued or new action in the future. When the feedback you give is well received, both you and the receiver feel okay about yourselves and your relationship. Upsetting feedback triggers defensiveness in the receiver and frustrates the socially aware feedback giver.

If you are skilled at giving effective feedback, your feedback is more likely to be well received. People will generally hold you in high regard, seek you out for wise counsel, trust you, and want to work for and with you. On the other hand, if you are weak in this skill, people will generally lack clarity about your expectations and intent, they will be hurt or angry about how you treat them, and they will be reluctant to seek your counsel, solicit your input, confide in you, or keep you informed.

You can make performance reviews win-win for all the stakeholders if you understand how and when to use different types of feedback, if you can combine different types of feedback for maximum benefit, and if your feedback engages, informs, empowers, and inspires employees.

How It's Done

In order to provide performance review feedback that will be well received, you need to understand three feedback principles, four different types of feedback and when to use them, and the framework for a feedback message. The rest is practice.

Feedback Principles

The first feedback principle is that the feedback receiver determines how to react to the feedback. Whether consciously or unconsciously, the feedback receiver perceives your feedback in his or her own way, and then reacts to his or her perception. You can't "make" the receiver like or dislike the feedback. The same feedback message, delivered with the same words and the same tone of voice, can be perceived as helpful by one receiver and harmful by another. Some people can tolerate harsh, direct, negative feedback and immediately put the message to good use; their mental filters process the feedback in a useful way. Others can react to the harshness, directness, and negativity and be unable to put the message to good use; their mental filters process the feedback as threatening, ill intended, and destructive. To be effective at giving feedback, you need to increase the chances that the feedback you give will be well received rather than rejected. Said another way, a key to effective feedback is increasing the odds that the receiver will be in a receptive state of mind and, once the feedback has been given, feel good about you and him- or herself, feel informed and motivated, and be clear about future actions.

This leads to the second feedback principle: The feedback receiver is more likely to receive feedback well if it is not authoritative. This is about the differences between authority and autonomy, condescension and respect, and domination and collaboration. If the receiver perceives your feedback as coming from authority (meaning positional power; a commanding, dominating, or arrogant style; or self-centered thinking), he or she is more likely to make an adversarial response (defensive, argumentative, blaming someone else, challenging your data, etc.) or an overly accommodating response (passively tolerating or accepting what you say, complying but not really committing, holding in bad feelings that later show up in counterproductive actions). If your feedback is less authoritative, it is more likely to engage the receiver in a collaborative dialogue, the receiver is more likely to consciously or unconsciously decide to receive your feedback well, and the message will be effective at reinforcing or initiating action or at advancing the conversation in some constructive way. You will find more information on this in the section "A Closer Look at Authoritative Feedback."

The third feedback principle is that the feedback receiver cannot control the thoughts and feelings others experience or the actions they take in response to his or her behavior. It is based on the premise that people have a choice about how to react to things. This principle does not apply to the physical realities that result from an action. If an angry boss pushes an employee who then falls and breaks an arm, the boss is responsible for the fall and fracture, but the boss is not responsible for the particular thoughts, feelings, and subsequent actions of the employee; those are all subject to the employee's attitude and view of life. One employee might feel humiliated, while another might feel happy at the opportunity to exploit an industrial injury situation and seek revenge against the boss.

Different feedback givers may perceive and react to the receiver's behavior in different ways, and that influences the nature of the feedback they give. If, for example, three people give a new team leader feedback on how she conducted a meeting, one of them might say, "I felt free to bring anything up"; another might say, "I was frustrated by the lack of structure"; and the third might say, "I was fully engaged." The feedback receiver behaved the same way to all three people at the same time, yet their perceptions and responses were quite different. You will find more information on this in the section "A Closer Look at Impact Feedback."

Feedback Types

Virtually all feedback can be classified as one of four different types. Three of these types are authoritative, which risks eliciting resistance or passive compliance. The fourth type is informative and empowering in nature; it promotes collaboration. You will be more effective in performance reviews if you are proficient at using all four types of feedback at the right times and for the right reasons. The following are three types of authoritative feedback:

Directive. This type of feedback tells the feedback receiver what to do. For example, "Be sure people have finished their thoughts before you respond to them." Directive feedback can take the form of command, advice, advocacy, request, inquiry, or example. It is important in performance reviews to clarify goals and expectations, instruct, advise, coach, and train. But directive feedback is authoritative; the feedback giver assumes the authority of knowing what should be done, how it should be done, and why it should be done.

13

Contingency. This type of feedback notifies the receiver about a future consequence that depends on whether he or she does or does not do something. For example, "If you keep interrupting people in meetings, they will stop cooperating with you." Contingency feedback is important in performance reviews to demonstrate the consequences and importance of doing or not doing something, and it speaks to cause and effect. But contingency feedback is authoritative; the feedback giver assumes the authority of controlling or being able to predict effects or contingent consequences.

Attribution. This type of feedback describes the receiver, the receiver's actions, or the receiver's output in terms of a quality or label. For example, "You are a good communicator." Attribution feedback is important in performance reviews to indicate value or quality, and to classify the nature of actions and outputs. But attribution feedback is authoritative; the feedback giver assumes the authority of judging the value and nature of actions or outcomes.

Authoritative feedback is most effective when the receiver is in a receptive state of mind. That can be promoted by the fourth type of feedback, which informs receivers without exercising authority over what the receiver *should* do with the message. It describes impact.

Impact. This type of feedback informs the receiver about the effect his or her actions have had upon other people or the system in which they operate. For example, "Team members were confused, and I was frustrated." Impact feedback is important in performance reviews to inform the receiver about impacts of which he or she might otherwise be unaware. It is not authoritative; the feedback giver does not tell the receiver what to do, set forth a contingent consequence, or express a value judgment about the receiver or what the receiver has done. Instead, impact feedback informs receivers, empowers them to do whatever they want to do with the information, and thereby increases the chance that they will decide to embrace the message in a collaborative, responsible, and responsive manner.

Each of these four types of feedback is effective when used at the right time and for the right reasons, and they can be used in combination. This guidebook will help you understand when to use the different types of feedback, how to frame a complete feedback message, and how to practice the four types of feedback until you can effectively apply them.

A Closer Look at Authoritative Feedback

Now let's take a more detailed look at the three types of authoritative feedback: directive, contingency, and attribution.

Directive Feedback

This type of feedback is future oriented; it specifies a type of action for the receiver to take. Directive feedback tells the receiver what to do, what not to do, or what to do differently. In the story at the beginning of this guidebook, Ethan does this when he suggests that Brenda use different wording, like "symptoms" instead of "problem." Directive feedback can be delivered in six different styles (command, advice, advocacy, request, inquiry, and example), and a different tone or attitude can be used with each style (for example, harsh, warm, impatient, or easygoing).

Command. You can give directive feedback in the form of a command. Essentially, you are giving an order, making a demand, or instructing; this is telling the receiver what to do in the most literal sense.

- "Make priorities clearer to your direct reports."

You can enhance or emphasize command-style directive feedback by prefacing it with a rationale (such as "I would appreciate it if..." or "Things would run more smoothly if...") or with your expectations (such as "I expect you to…" or "It is my understanding that you will…").

Advice. You can structure your directive feedback as advice or a recommendation. Advising leaves the final decision up to the feedback receiver; it feels less authoritative to the receiver than a command.

- "I would suggest that you make priorities clearer to your direct reports."

Advocacy. You can structure your directive feedback as advocacy. When advocating, you speak in favor of or promote a new or different action. It is a lot like advice; the difference is that advice feels a little more personal to the receiver than advocacy. Advice emphasizes the receiver more than the action. Advocacy emphasizes the action more than the receiver.

- "Direct reports are more aligned when you make priorities clearer to them."

Request. You can structure your directive feedback as a request. The message is basically the same as telling the receiver what to do, but you are asking rather than telling. A request is less authoritative than a command.

- "How about making priorities clearer to your direct reports?"

Inquiry. You can structure your directive feedback as an inquiry. The feedback giver asks the receiver to consider options or possibilities. It implies that the receiver has a choice; the prescribed action appears optional, so it feels less authoritative to the receiver.

- "Are there ways to make priorities clearer to your direct reports?"

16

Example. You can structure your directive feedback as an example. In this case, the feedback giver uses a story to convey the message.

- "Let me tell you about an experience that taught me to make priorities clearer to my direct reports."

Contingency Feedback

In this type of feedback, givers alert receivers to the likely or certain consequences of their doing or not doing something. Ethan does this when he tells Brenda that if she does not improve her reputation with the staff, he will be forced to make some changes. The consequences to feedback receivers are contingent on the action in question. While the emphasis is on the contingent consequence, there is still a message telling feedback receivers what to do:

- "If you work on this team, you'll get visibility." (Prescriptive message: "Be on the team." Consequence: visibility.)

Attribution Feedback

In this type of feedback, givers attribute a quality to the receiver or something the receiver has done. Ethan does this when he describes Brenda as "one of the sharpest problem solvers on the team." In order to convey an attribution, we have to pass judgment on the feedback receiver or on what the feedback receiver has done or not done. For example:

- "You're good with people." (Quality attributed to the receiver: good with people. Prescriptive message embedded in this attribution: "Keep doing what you are doing with people.")

Forms of Directive Feedback

The receiver is likely to experience the feedback as...	Form	Definition
More Controlling ↑↓ Less Controlling	Command	Tell the receiver what to do.
	Advice	Recommend what the receiver should do.
	Advocacy	Promote an action that the receiver should do.
	Request	Ask the receiver to do something.
	Inquiry	Ask the receiver to consider an option.
	Example	Use a story to illustrate what the receiver should do.

A Closer Look at Impact Feedback

Impact feedback describes reactions to or outcomes stemming from the receiver's actions. This feature of impact feedback, more than anything else, differentiates it from authoritative feedback—it is not about the feedback receiver. Impact feedback is about reaction to or consequences of what the feedback receiver has done or not done.

Good impact statements enable feedback receivers to be aware of reactions others are having to their behavior or things happening in the organization that are connected to their behavior. This can be informative if the receiver is unaware of the reactions or consequences, and that information can empower the receiver to consider other alternatives. You can inform the receiver of three types of impact:

Your own thoughts and feelings, or actions you have taken

- "I described your achievement to my boss."

The reactions of third parties that you observe or are reported to you

- "I noticed that the team members started moving around in their seats and shuffling papers."

Circumstances in the organization

- "Hospital infection rates have declined 3 percent."

Be sure that your impact statements really are about impact. Consider the following:

- "I noticed that you were friendly."
  "Friendly" is an attribution; it reveals a judgment by the feedback giver, friendly versus not friendly. An impact alternative is "I felt at ease."

Think back now to the third feedback principle: The feedback receiver cannot control the thoughts and feelings others experience or the actions they take in response to his or her behavior. Impact feedback never attributes blame or responsibility to the receiver for the impact. That is a key to impact feedback—not being authoritative. Once you attribute blame or responsibility to the receiver, you increase the probability that the receiver will become defensive, upset, or disengaged. Be careful with words like *made, caused*, and *because* when making an impact statement. These words are often used to attribute blame. Consider this example:

19

- "When you did not answer my question, it made me angry."

The feedback giver is blaming the behavior (not answering the question) for his or her feeling of anger, instead of taking the responsibility for perceiving the behavior, reacting to that perception, and experiencing the feeling of anger. Using *made* in this example attributes blame and conveys the embedded message that the feedback giver had no choice in the matter, that anger was the only possible response.

For this example, appropriate impact feedback would be "When you did not answer my question, I felt angry" or "I got angry when you did not answer my question." This may seem like a pretty subtle difference, and it is. But it's worth making a subtle change in order to increase the probability that your feedback will be well received.

CCL's SBI Model

For a long time, CCL has recognized the value of giving feedback in the form of situation, behavior, and impact. Here are some examples of that model in action:

- "Chris, at the end of the team meeting this morning (situation), you gave a summary of the key action steps we had discussed (behavior). I was really glad you did that (impact on me), and it seemed to bring a good sense of closure to the meeting (impact on the process)." (Instead of "Chris, you were really effective in the team meeting today.")

- "Pat, during our conference call yesterday afternoon (situation), I noticed that you interrupted others and me on several occasions (behavior). I felt frustrated at times (impact on me), and I noticed that the others started arguing and cutting each other off (impact on others)." (Instead of "Pat, you were really rude yesterday.")

Fitting Impact Terms to the Receiver

It is good practice to consider the perspective of the feedback receiver. Based on individual predispositions and gender, cultural, ethnic, religious, and educational differences (among others), people may be more receptive to one choice of words than another. Some people are receptive to talking about feelings more than others; some people are more comfortable with "getting personal" while others prefer to keep things impersonal or "all business." As you advance in your feedback skills, you will become more flexible in your choice of impact words, learning to use words that will be well received by the person to whom you deliver feedback.

Consider this example: Your direct report, a project leader, has not made project goals clear to team members. A fairly personal impact statement might be "Team members are upset" or "Team members are complaining." Since some people might take that too personally, you might use less personal terms, like "Team members are concerned" or "Team members have expressed uncertainty." You can be even less personal by saying something like "Team efforts appear unfocused" or "Team productivity is not what it could be."

Comparing Authoritative and Impact Feedback

Note three critical qualities of authoritative types of feedback (directive, contingency, and attribution) as opposed to impact feedback: it is judgmental, prescriptive, and focused on the feedback receiver.

In giving authoritative feedback, you must make a determination about good or bad, right or wrong. Impact feedback, however, is quite different. It does not judge the receiver or the receiver's actions. Instead, impact feedback is nonjudgmental and informative. It describes reactions to and consequences of the actions of the receiver.

Authoritative feedback prescribes behavior. Based on a judgment of what is preferred or better, the feedback message contains an explicit or implicit prescription for how to act, what to do, or how things should be. Impact feedback contains no prescription. It is empowering; it leaves the receiver free to choose a course of action rather than comply or defy the prescription.

Further, authoritative feedback focuses on the receiver. One could say you are pointing your finger at the receiver. It is either about the receiver personally (*"You* did this" or *"You* did not do that"*) or about the result of what the receiver has done (*"It* is good" or *"It* is bad."). Impact feedback focuses on the giver, third parties, or the organization. It is about disclosure, not accusation.

Impact	Authoritative
Informative	Judgmental
Empowering	Prescriptive
Objective	Subjective
Less threatening	More threatening
About feedback giver, third party, or organization	About feedback receiver
Likely to evoke...	*Likely to evoke...*
Commitment	Compliance
Collaboration	Resistance
Cooperation	Passivity
Initiative	Subterfuge

When to Use Authoritative and Impact Feedback

Impact feedback works well when the receiver cares about the impact. That is, the receiver is likely to respect or appreciate the information and be predisposed to strive to do the best thing about it. That might mean hearing the feedback and then expressing appreciation, apologizing, initiating action without guidance, or asking for more information. If a receiver has a "that's your problem," "toughen up," "that's not my fault," or "so what?" attitude, impact feedback does not help and may make things worse. Fortunately, people often do care, and when they do, impact feedback triggers receptivity for more information or opens a dialogue. Often a receiver will request guidance and suggestions, opening the door for authoritative feedback.

Combining impact feedback with authoritative feedback is very effective. Impact feedback is a great tool for creating interest or receptivity. Impact feedback alerts the receiver to why something is important. Hopefully, it will have the effect of eliciting a response inside the receiver along the lines of "If my behavior had that impact, maybe I should keep doing it" or "If what I did can have that sort of impact, maybe I should do less of it or do something different." In either case, the receiver might then be interested in knowing more about the specifics of what he or she did, the nature of the impact, and options for future behavior. The impact has thus engaged the receiver in discussion and perhaps problem solving. And because impact feedback is not prescriptive or judgmental, the receiver's engagement is voluntary, and further conversation is at the receiver's initiative as much as the feedback giver's. Receptivity has been encouraged. The receiver may now want your guidance, which you can give in the form of one of the authoritative types of feedback.

Keep this in mind if you plan to combine types of feedback: Trust impact to do the job in most cases. You will be amazed by what constructive things people will do with well-delivered impact feedback. They may ask for guidance. They may suggest a new course of behavior. Give the feedback receiver an opportunity to digest the impact and respond to it before you offer authoritative input. Feedback receivers may then ask for suggestions or offer suggestions themselves. If not, ask if they want a suggestion before offering one.

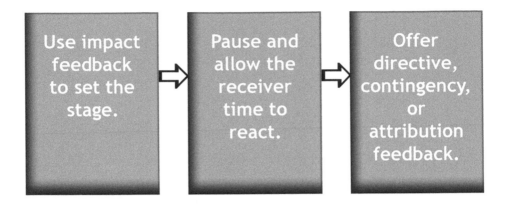

Pausing after giving impact feedback may be the hardest part of this process. Leaders and managers often say that they feel they have not done enough when they "just give impact." Certainly, in many cases, more information will be needed. But develop the self-discipline to wait after giving brief, crisp impact feedback. Wait for the receiver to respond in some way, and that will tell you your next step. Consider these examples to an impact statement like "I am frustrated by [something the receiver did]."

Receiver's Response	Your Next Move
"What was frustrating about that?"	Answer the question and then pause again. Strive not to be judgmental or prescriptive yet.
"I know I do that sometimes, and I am trying to break the habit."	Thank the receiver for hearing you out. Ask if there is any way you can be supportive. Stop short of authoritative feedback.
"I'm really sorry about that, but I don't know how else to handle this situation."	Ask if the receiver wants some suggestions and provide them if the answer is yes.

Framework for a Feedback Message

While the core of performance feedback is impact and authoritative messages, the effectiveness of feedback is affected by how well you frame the core feedback message when delivering it. The framework has three components that support the core feedback message: intent, situation, and behavior.

Intent

If you don't tell the feedback receiver why you are giving feedback, he or she will invent a reason. This takes us back to the first feedback principle: The feedback receiver determines how to react to the feedback. This tendency among feedback receivers is practically universal. As feedback is coming their way, receivers consciously or unconsciously speculate about why you are giving it, or they make up a story about your motivations, or they form a judgment of you based on how they feel about the feedback. Your best course of action is to make your intent clear in the beginning so the receiver focuses on the feedback and not on you.

Intent can be implicit or explicit. If the feedback receiver knows you well enough and the process of giving feedback has been well established, you need not make your intent explicit every time. However, when there is any chance of your intent being misinterpreted, you are wise to make it explicit. For example:

- "In order to solve some problems that have come to my attention, I would like to offer some feedback."

Situation

Feedback is about something the receiver did, or did not do, in a context of time, place, and circumstance. In cases where that context is not self-evident, describing it is critical to making feedback effective and well received. Context often determines what behavior is appropriate and what is not. In one meeting an individual should remain fairly silent and attend to the proceedings; in another meeting the same individual should speak up and take a stand. When you adequately describe the context, feedback receivers understand or remember when and where they were at the time, and what variable conditions were in play that would call for the expression or inhibition of certain behavior. For example:

- "When you presented our March sales figures to the senior management team last Thursday…"

When you describe the context, be specific about the time and place. Describe the circumstances: who was there, the agenda, and what other people were doing. Check to determine whether the receiver remembers the situation.

Behavior

Feedback givers describe feedback receivers' observable behaviors—things that could be captured through audio or video recording. Behaviors that can be recorded are sounds (such as words, tone of voice, groans, sighs) and actions (such as body language, gestures, facial expressions, and rolling the eyes). Good behavioral descriptions enable feedback receivers to know exactly what they did that had impact on others. For example:

- "You provided details when making your point, and you answered questions directly."

When you describe behavior, be sure to use action verbs instead of verbs of being like *is* and *are*. Be concrete and avoid abstractions. Doing so avoids confusion and increases clarity about your message.

Using concrete, behavioral terms is more challenging than you might think. We are so accustomed to using abstractions to communicate that we don't realize it, and therefore we don't realize that people may interpret our abstractions differently than we do. Moreover, abstractions that describe behavior are attributions, so we are setting up authoritative feedback whenever we use them.

Use the worksheet on pages 28–29 to practice recognizing concrete descriptions of behavior.

Feedback Follow-Up

Remember Ethan, whose authoritative feedback was not well received? His follow-up conversation with Brenda went like this:

Ethan was committed to breaking the stalemate with Brenda and salvaging her relationship with the staff at the health center. He planned a different approach for their follow-up conversation the next week. He started the meeting by asking Brenda if she had any thoughts or reactions to their previous conversation, now that she'd had a week to think about it. Ethan was hoping to create a more collaborative atmosphere. "I still don't get why you are confronting *me*," Brenda started. "If the providers would just follow procedures, there would be no problem!"

"You are right about that, Brenda," Ethan responded. "You have told them that, and still the problem is not solved. What if it is not about the content of your message, but more about the way the message is sent and how they interpret it? The providers say they end up feeling put down and ridiculed by the way you speak to them. Do you want them to feel that way?"

Brenda shifted in her seat and looked irritated. "Of course not, but that's their problem. I'm just giving them the facts."

"True," Ethan replied, "but is that the impact you want to have on them?"

"Well, no. I said that."

"What kind of impact would you like to have on them?" Ethan asked.

"I'd just as soon they had no reaction except to follow procedures."

"So perhaps wording things a little differently would create that impact and make your life easier," Ethan continued.

"I suppose you are right, but I'm not sure how to word it better," Brenda replied, looking a little less irritated.

Behavior or Not Behavior: That Is the Question

Use a check mark to classify each item as Behavior or Not Behavior. Summarize your reasoning in the Why column. Then see the key at the bottom of page 29.

Item	Behavior	Not Behavior	Why
1. You were aggressive.			
2. You suggested we do a matrix to sort out the options.			
3. You invited people to express their opinions and asked follow-up questions.			
4. You are not skilled at collaboration.			

Item	Behavior	Not Behavior	Why
5. You described the process step by step.			
6. You interrupted her several times.			
7. Your attitude was threatening.			
8. You started the meeting by criticizing the team for its performance.			
9. You spoke twice during the 40-minute meeting.			

Key: Items 2, 3, 5, 6, 8, and 9 are behaviors. Items 1, 4, and 7 are not.

Ethan recognized that the conversation finally had taken a turn for the better. Brenda seemed to understand that she had a choice of behaviors that would lead to different impacts. Better yet, there was an implied request for assistance in her last statement. But Ethan knew not to get ahead of Brenda. He had to take it slow and keep pace with her. "I think that's pretty natural. We all have our ways of doing things that are second nature to us. Doing things differently is always a learning curve, and it can help people to get coaching on new approaches, just as you probably had teachers and coaches that helped you master different aspects of information technology." Ethan wanted Brenda to see that reaching out for help is as appropriate in behavioral matters as it is with technical skills.

Brenda's shift to a more collaborative posture was quick. "What would you suggest?" she asked. Now she was receptive to the kind of authoritative feedback Ethan had given a week earlier. He could make suggestions (directive), make predictions (contingency), and use qualitative statements and labels (attribution). The difference was that Brenda now understood why the authoritative feedback was valuable to her. Once she understood that her behavior had an undesirable impact on others, which then became an obstacle to the results she wanted (their following procedures), she was empowered to seek options and therefore more receptive.

Suggested Readings

Buron, R. J., & McDonald-Mann, D. (1999). *Giving feedback to subordinates*. Greensboro, NC: Center for Creative Leadership.

Hoppe, M. H. (2006). *Active listening: Improve your ability to listen and lead*. Greensboro, NC: Center for Creative Leadership.

Kirkland, K., & Manoogian, S. (1998). *Ongoing feedback: How to get it, how to use it*. Greensboro, NC: Center for Creative Leadership.

Popejoy, B., & McManigle, B. J. (2002). *Managing conflict with direct reports*. Greensboro, NC: Center for Creative Leadership.

Smith, R., & Campbell, M. (2011). *Talent conversations: What they are, why they're crucial, and how to do them right.* Greensboro, NC: Center for Creative Leadership.

Ting, S., & Scisco, P. (Eds.). (2006). *The CCL handbook of coaching: A guide for the leader coach.* San Francisco: Jossey-Bass.

Weitzel, S. R. (2000). *Feedback that works: How to build and deliver your message.* Greensboro, NC: Center for Creative Leadership.

Background

For many years, the Center for Creative Leadership has encouraged people to give feedback in the form of situation, behavior, and impact. Many leaders and managers have told us that other forms of feedback are also necessary, especially in performance reviews when the focus is on how well an organizational member has been doing and on setting goals for future behavior. It became clear to us, therefore, that impact feedback will be more useful to leaders and managers as a choice among options, with its own strategic and tactical strengths and weaknesses like the others. This realization led to the study of the performance review process and deliberation about the forms of feedback that play an important role in that process.

Key Point Summary

Effective feedback is one of the most important components of successful performance reviews. Feedback is important assessment data that either supports continuing to perform in some manner or targets a desirable change. To provide performance review feedback that will be well received, you need to understand three feedback principles, four different types of feedback and when to use them, and the framework for a feedback message. The rest is practice.

31

The first feedback principle is that the feedback receiver determines how to react to the feedback. The second feedback principle is that the feedback receiver is more likely to receive feedback well if it is not authoritative. The third feedback principle is that the feedback receiver cannot control the thoughts and feelings others experience or the actions they take in response to his or her behavior.

Virtually all feedback can be classified as one of four different types. Three of these types are authoritative: directive, contingency, and attribution. Directive feedback tells the feedback receiver what to do. It can be delivered in six different styles that range from more controlling to less controlling: command, advice, advocacy, request, inquiry, and example. Contingency feedback notifies the receiver about a future consequence that depends on whether he or she does or does not do something. Attribution feedback describes the receiver, the receiver's actions, or the receiver's output in terms of a quality or label. The fourth type of feedback, impact, informs the receiver about the effect his or her actions have had upon other people or the system in which they operate. You will be more effective in performance reviews if you are proficient at using all four types of feedback at the right times and for the right reasons.

While the core of performance feedback is impact and authoritative messages, the effectiveness of feedback is affected by how well you frame the core feedback message when delivering it. The framework has three components that support the core feedback message: intent, situation, and behavior.

Ordering Information

CPSIA information can be obtained
at www.ICGtesting.com
Printed in the USA
BVHW02s0018140518
515697BV00004BA/5/P